Common Core Reading Edition
1st Grade
Workbook Series

apple

\\ˈa-pəl\\

apple

balloon

\bə-ˈlün\

balloon

crocodile

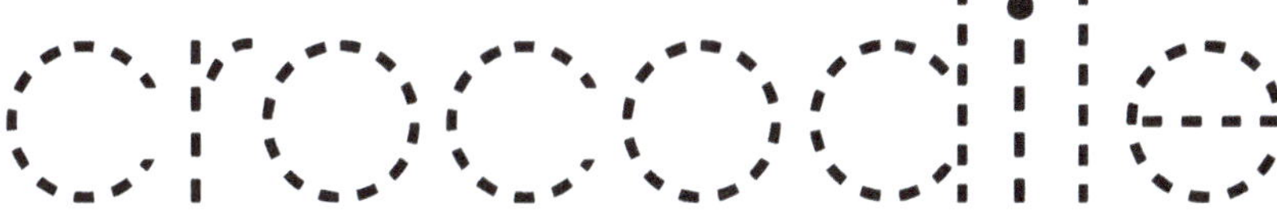

\\ˈkrä-kə-ˌdī(-ə)l\\

crocodile

dog

\\'do\u0307g, 'da\u0308g\\

elephant

\ˈe-lə-fənt\

flamingo

\flə-ˈmiŋ-(ˌ)gō\

flamingo

giraffe

\jə-ˈraf\

hippo

\\'hi-(ˌ)pō\\

hippo

ice cream

\ˌīs-ˈkrēm, ˈīs-ˌ \

ice cream

jam

\\'jam\\

jam

kite

\\'kīt\\

kite

lion

\ˈlī-ən\

lion

monkey

\ˈməŋ-kē\

nail

\\'nāl\\

nail

owl

\\\'au̇(-ə)l\\

penguin

\ˈpen-gwən, ˈpeŋ-\

penguin

queen

\\'kwēn\\

queen

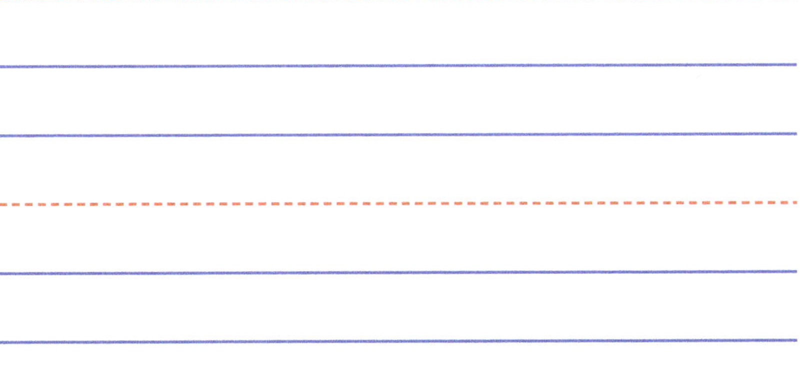

rabbit

\\'ra-bət\\

rabbit

sun

\ˈsən\

sun

tiger

\\'tī-gər\

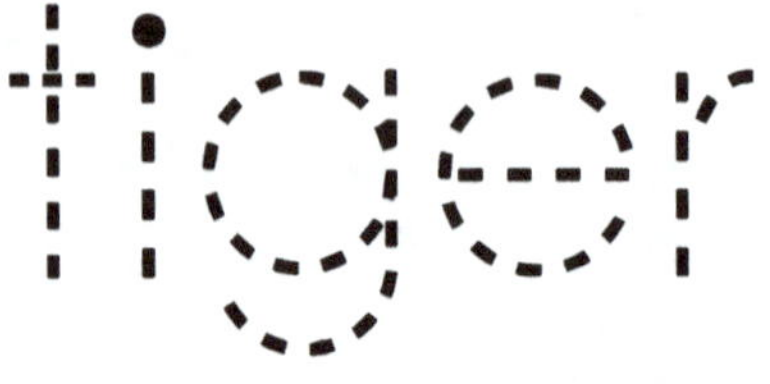

umbrella

\ ˌəm-ˈbre-lə, ˈəm-ˌ \

umbrella

violin

\ˌvī-ə-ˈlin\

worm

\\ˈwərm\\

worm

x-ray

\\ˈeks-ˌrā\\

yoyo

\\'yō-(ˌ)yō\\

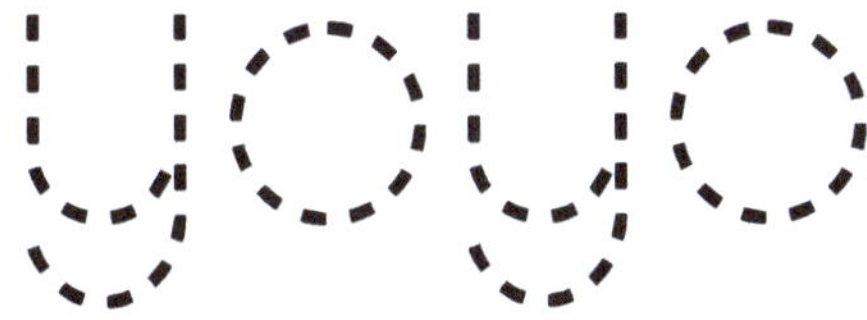

zebra

\\'zē-brə, 'ze-\\

There is a new swimming pool park in the next city. My family and I will go there over the weekend.

It has water slides and water inflatables. The slides are scary at first. But, when you tried it, you'll surely have fun and will try again.

Another pool make its own waves. There are big and small waves. Kids and kids alike love to surf in the big waves. It is really fun!

On Sundays, the park can be crowded. Familes of the city and the nearby go to the park and swim.

The park also has a snack bar where we can buy ice cream, junkfoods and other snacks.

The pool park does not allow pets, however, you can leave them outside since they also have a pet center.

Everyone loves the new pool park!